At School

by Lucy Long

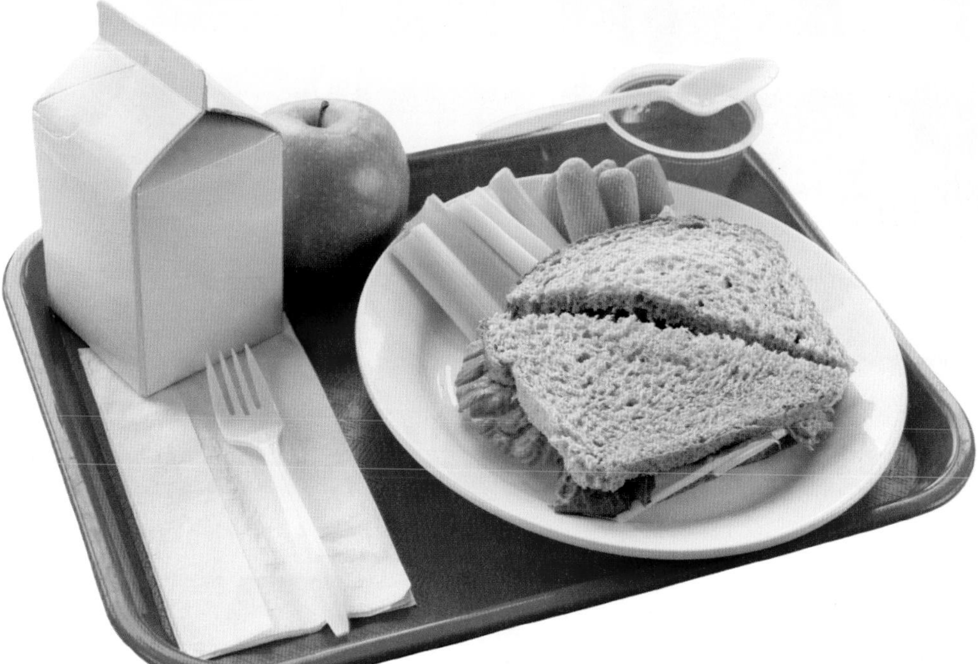

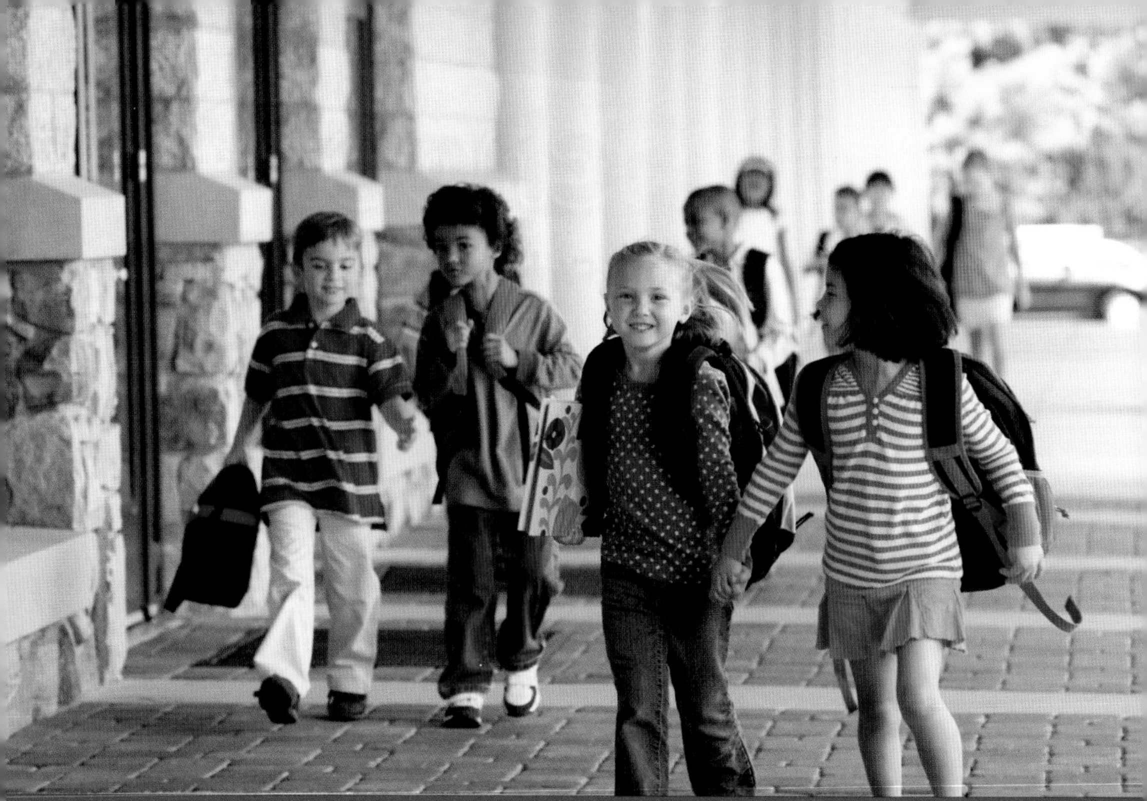

We see the 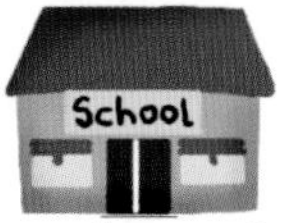

.

school

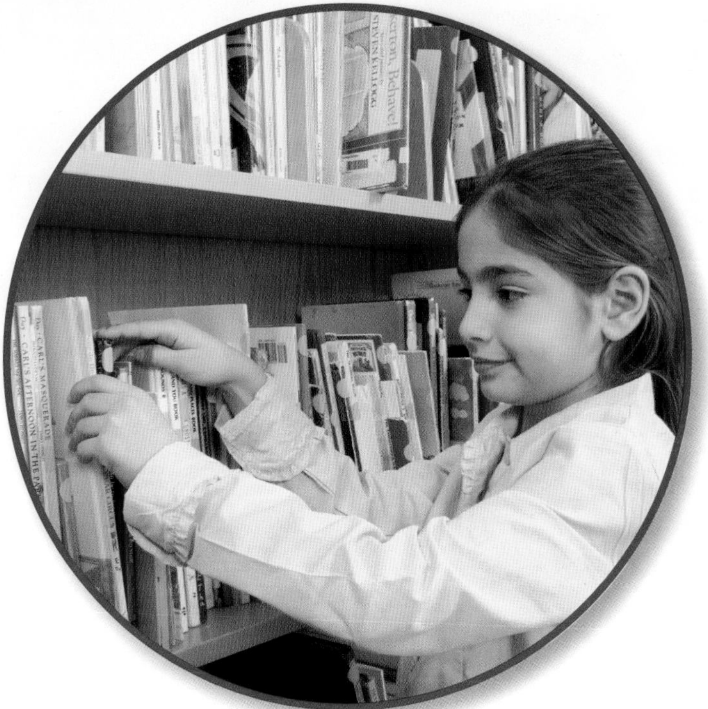

We see the 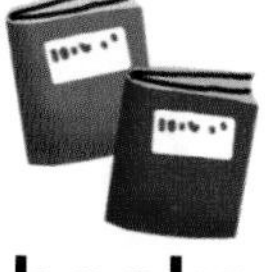 .

books

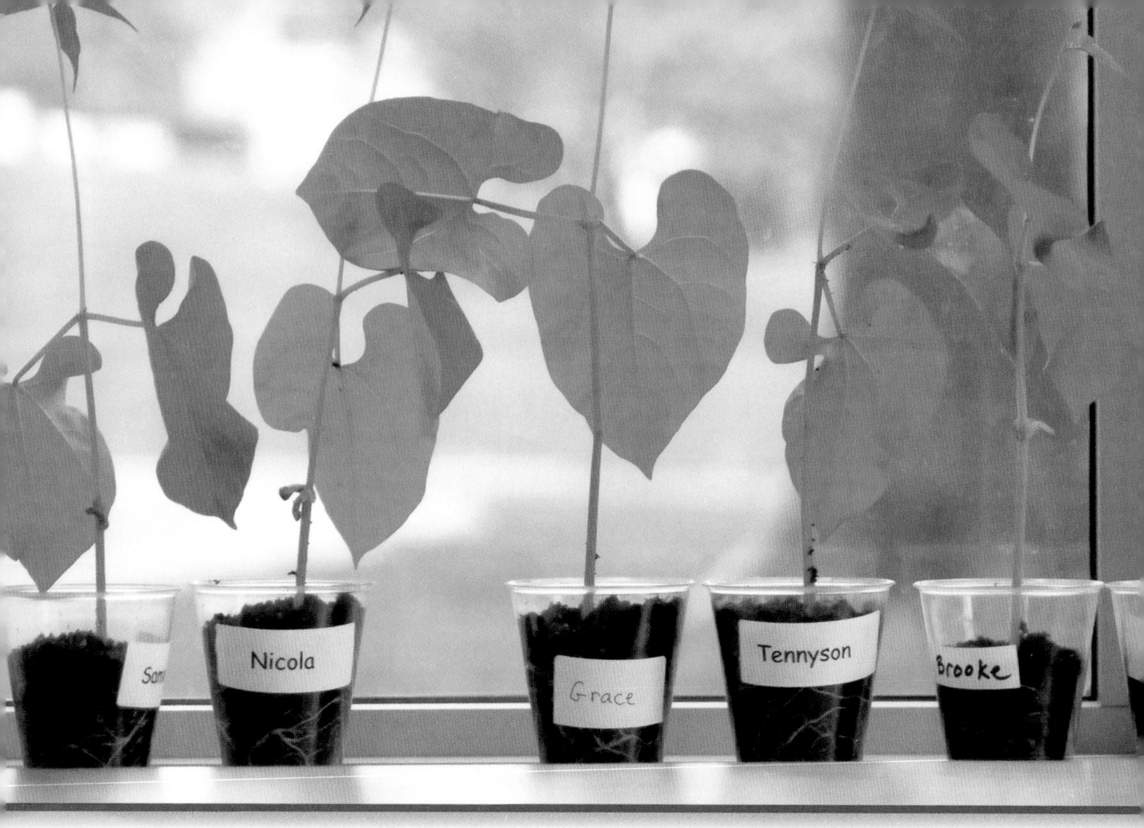

We see the 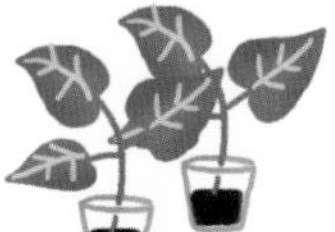 .

plants

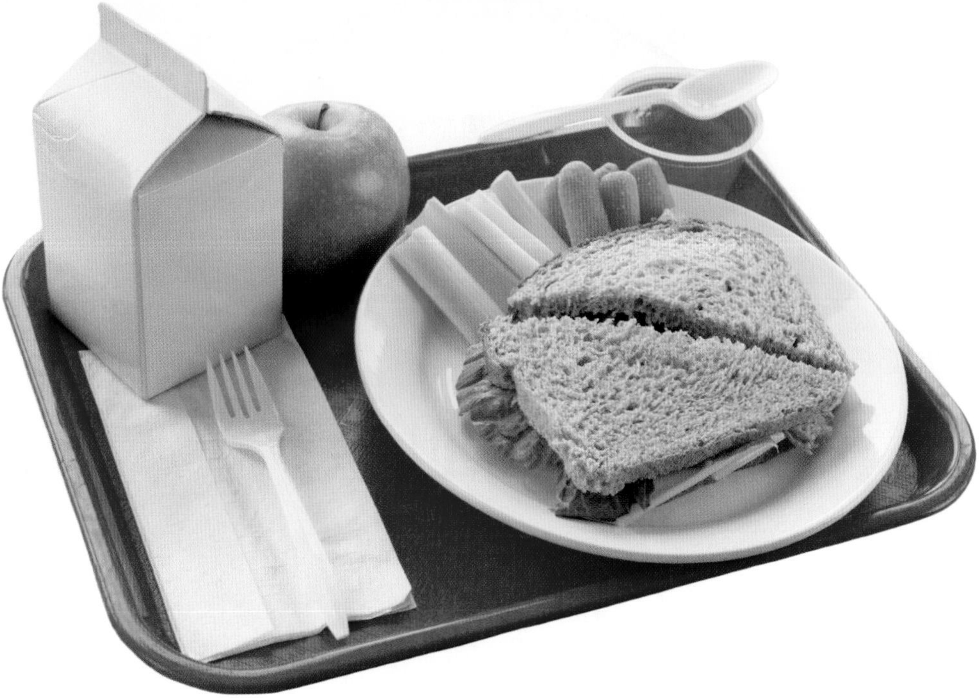

We see the 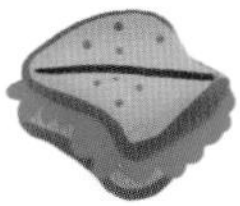 .

sandwich

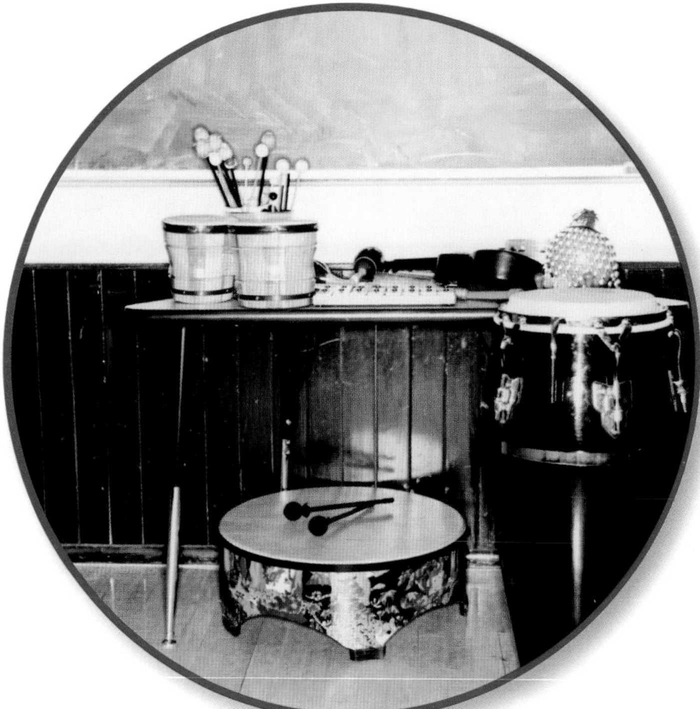

We see the 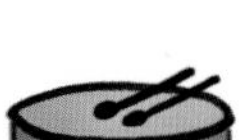.

drum

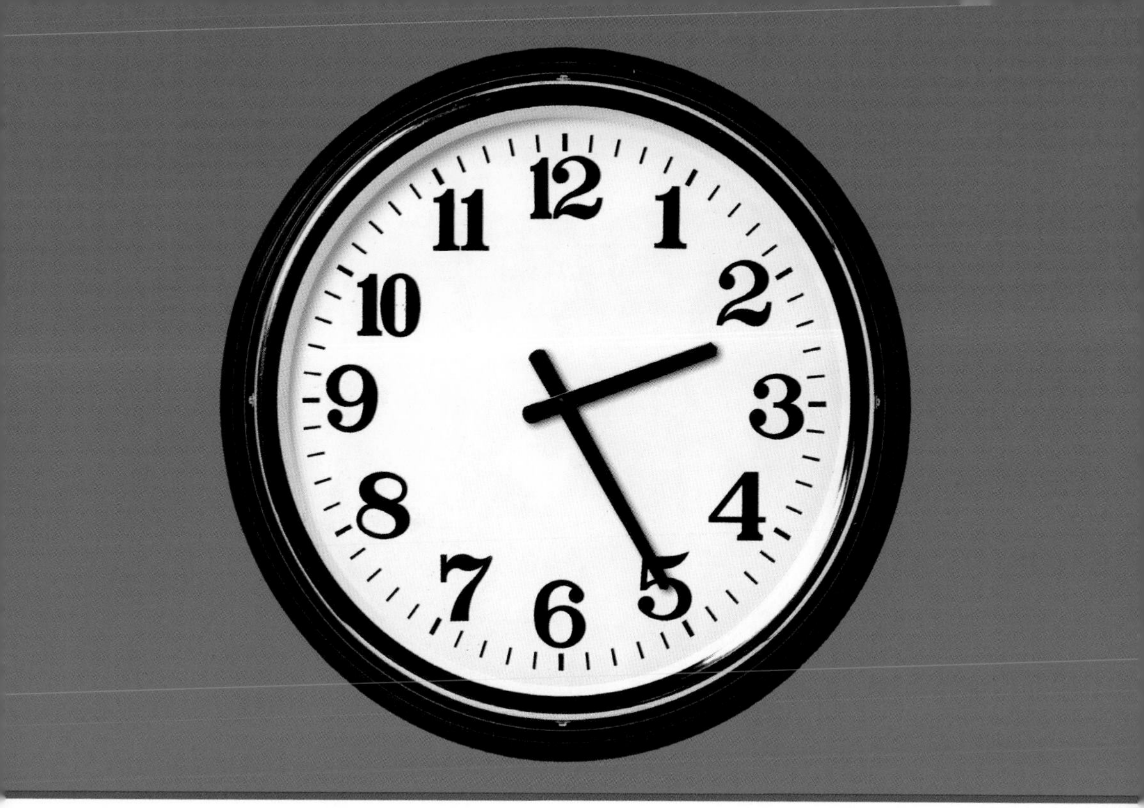

We see the 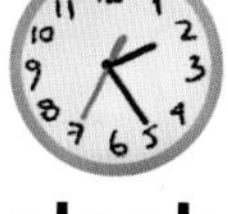 .

clock

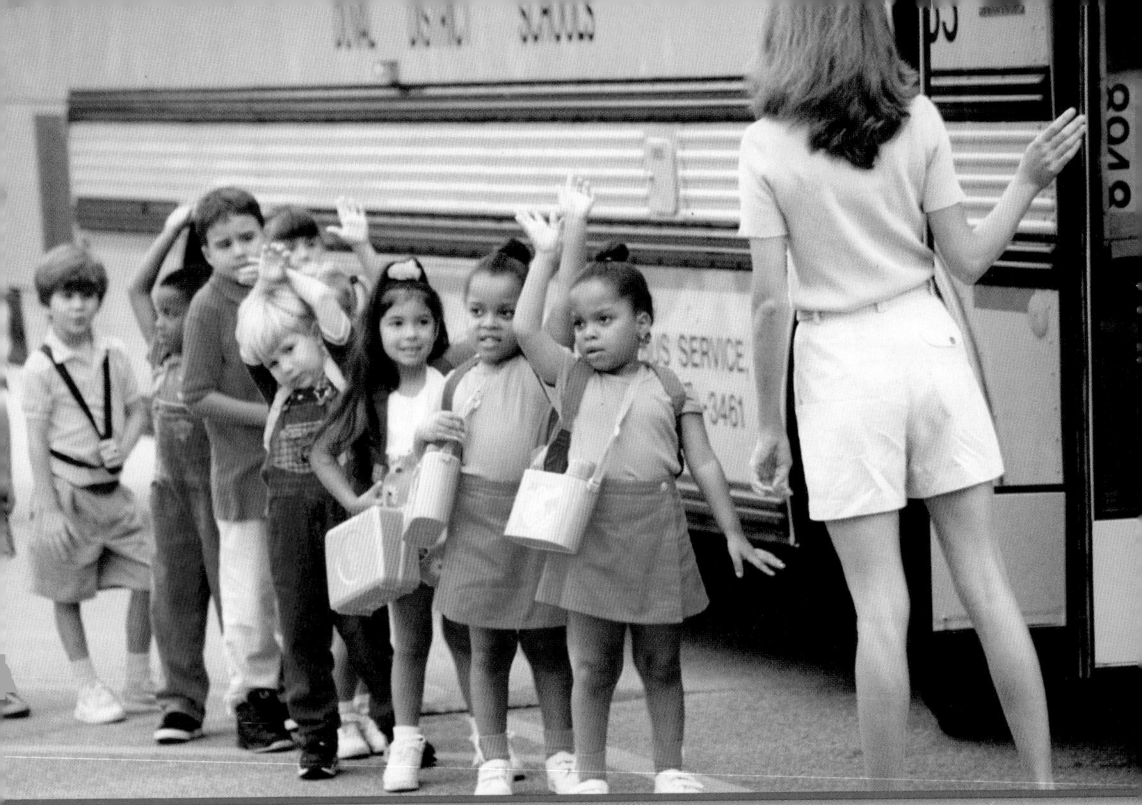

We see the 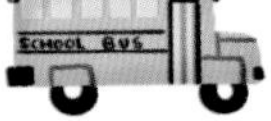

.

bus